PACKAGE DEAL

Real Deal bible studies

family issues

AUTHORS

Bill Ameiss

Eric Dauber

Tom Doyle

Chris Drager

Dennis Durham

Mark Etter

Gretchen Foth

Tim Frusti

Jim Gimbel

Diane Grebing

Cheryl Honoree

Joan Lilley

Jim Ollhoff

Cindy Wheeler

EDITOR

Mark Sengele

CONCORDIA PUBLISHING HOUSE · SAINT LOUIS

Copyright © 2003 by Concordia Publishing House, 3558 S. Jefferson Avenue, St. Louis, MO 63118-3968. Portions of this material originally published by Concordia Publishing House, copyright © 1993, 1994, 1995.

Your comments and suggestions concerning the material are appreciated. Please write the Editor of Youth Materials, Concordia Publishing House, 3558 S. Jefferson Avenue, St. Louis, MO 63118-3968

This publication may also be available in braille, in large print, or on cassette tape for the visually impaired. Please allow 8 to 12 weeks for delivery. Write to Library for the Blind, 1333 S. Kirkwood Road, St. Louis, MO 63122-7295; call 1-800-433-3954, ext. 1322; or e-mail to blind.library@lcms.org.

Scripture quotations are taken from the HOLY BIBLE, NEW INTERNATIONAL VERSION®. NIV®. Copyright © 1973, 1978, 1984 by International Bible Society. Used by permission of Zondervan Publishing House. All rights reserved.

Manufactured in the United States of America.

1 2 3 4 5 6 7 8 9 10   12 11 10 09 08 07 06 05 04 03

table of contents

iNTRODUCTION

WELCOME TO THE REAL DEAL SERIES!

Welcome to the Real Deal! Each of the books in this series presents 12 lessons that focus on the Gospel and the Word of God, the Real Deal. Each book in the series has a theme around which the lessons are organized. (For an outline of the Real Deal Series, look inside the back cover of this book.)

* ***The topics*** *are real. Each lesson deals with real issues in the lives of young people and is grounded in God's Word.*

* ***The leader's materials*** *are easy to use. Each lesson is completely outlined and designed for real success in teaching. Leader's directions are clear and easy to follow. Materials needed for teaching are easily obtained. Many lessons contain additional materials for times when students finish quickly.*

* ***Student pages*** *are reproducible so teachers can copy the number they really need.*

* *And, finally, the **power of the Gospel** is at the core of every study. Students will see God's Word as the real source of information for their everyday lives.*

ABOUT THIS BOOK

Package Deal

Each of the 12 studies in this book deals with family issues that many young people face. Many of these issues can be very sensitive for young people to deal with. Use care in your approach to each study so that God's truths remain objective and your care for each student becomes personalized.

The studies are designed for use with students in the ninth through twelfth grades. More mature junior high students may also benefit from these studies. Each study is a complete unit. Lessons may be used in any order. While designed for the typical one-hour Bible class, these studies may be adapted for other youth ministry settings. For example, selected studies could form the core of material for a youth night or retreat.

PREPARING TO TEACH

Each lesson has a *Lesson Focus* and a *Gospel Focus* statement at the beginning. These help the leader understand the lesson topic and direction.

The *Lesson Outline* provides a quick look at the study and a list of materials needed for each segment of the lesson.

The *Lesson Activities* include large- and small-group discussion, opportunities for individual study, and active-learning suggestions.

Most lessons also contain background information to assist the leader in preparing for the class time. Class leaders should review the entire lesson in advance of the class time.

It is assumed that the Bible class leader will have the usual basic classroom equipment and supplies available—pencils or pens for each student, blank paper (and occasionally tape or marking pens), and a chalkboard or its equivalent (white board, overhead transparency projector, or newsprint pad and easel) with corresponding markers or chalk. Encourage the students to bring their own Bibles. Then they can mark useful passages and make notes to guide their personal Bible study and reference. Do provide additional Bibles, however, for visitors or students who do not bring one. The appropriate Student Page should be copied in a quantity sufficient for the class and distributed at the time indicated in the leader's notes.

The studies are outlined completely in the leader's notes, including a suggested length of time recommended for each section of the study. The suggested times will total 50–60 minutes, the maximum amount most Sunday-morning Bible classes have available. Each session begins with an opening activity that may or may not be indicated on the Student Page. Teachers who regularly begin with prayer should include it before the opening activity. Most other parts of the study, except the closing prayer, are indicated both in the Leader Guide and on the Student Page.

An average class size of 10 students is assumed. To facilitate discussion, especially when your class is larger than average, it is recommended to conduct much of the discussion in smaller groups—pairs, triads, or groups of no more than five or six. Instructions to that effect are often included in the guide. If your class is small, you are already a small group and can ignore any such suggestions.

Some lessons contain bonus suggestions. Use these when the study progresses more quickly than expected, when your normal session exceeds 50–60 minutes, or when a suggested activity doesn't work with your group. They can also be used during the week.

Of course, the leader is encouraged to review the study thoroughly, well in advance of its presentation. Then the materials can be tailored to your individual students' needs and preferences as well as your own preferred teaching style.

TIPS FOR LEADERS OF YOUTH BIBLE STUDIES

One challenge of leading a youth Bible study is the need for relevant, Christ-centered, effective study material. An equal challenge is growing in one's ability to teach and lead effectively. While the studies in the Real Deal Series are intended to meet the first challenge, the material in this section is intended to help you meet the second challenge.

Skim this section for ideas that spark your interest, or read it completely. Either way, you'll find support to help young people grow in God's Word.

BEGIN WITH THE END IN MIND

A common complaint among young people is that Bible study is irrelevant and boring. As the leader, you have the opportunity to ensure that every study impacts the lives of your students. You can help it become relevant and interesting to them. Stated simply, begin with the end in mind.

Life application is almost always the last section of a study. If time is short, if things get sidetracked, if you run late, the end of the class period usually suffers. You may be tempted to shorten or omit the life application—but don't. Doing so diminishes the effectiveness of the study.

So begin with the end in mind, knowing what you hope to accomplish as the Holy Spirit works in the lives of your students. You can then more easily reserve the necessary time so that, even if class time is short, the whole lesson is taught.

Study the end of your lesson plans carefully. Memorize the life-application activities. Know where you're going. Your lessons will be more effective, and your students will be more interested.

GET TO KNOW YOUR STUDENTS

Relevant teaching and good relationships are to some degree a function of your personal knowledge of the students you teach. The more you know about them, the easier the task of helping them grow.

One director of Christian education keeps careful track of birthdays among the young people in his congregation. The week before each birthday, he prays for the individual. He makes contact by phone or in person to extend personal wishes. Consider discussing birthday plans or wishes, giving a small gift, or treating the high school student to an outing for an ice-cream sundae and conversation.

Another teacher keeps a spiral notebook with a page for each student who attends her class. Each week after class, she adds notes about each student present that day. What concerns did they seem to have? What new information did they share? What helpful or disruptive actions did she notice? (Use this weekly review to guide your prayers for your students. It may also stimulate occasional phone calls sharing thanks for good class participation or to remind students of your support for them.)

FOLLOW-UP IS THE KEY TO BUILDING ATTENDANCE

Do you wish yours was a growing, dynamic Bible class with 100 percent attendance every week? The best study material, even the most charismatic leader, cannot guarantee it. These things will certainly help. So will prayer, refreshments, and the power of the Holy Spirit.

There is another way that you can make a great impact on regular attendance. You can often reactivate absent students with a few minutes of follow-up each week. Here are some possibilities:

* Ask the class about absent students. *"I don't see _____ today—does anyone know if he/she is out of town?" The young people themselves often have better information than you.*

* Follow-up personally and promptly. *Touch base with two or three absentees. Skip the guilt-inducers, such as "Why weren't you in Bible class?" Focus on "I" messages, like "I missed you in class today." Tell the absentees you missed them. Mention next week's topic and sign off cheerfully; you may be surprised at the results.*

* Involve active students in the process. *Enlist a few students to remind friends of the Bible class time, topics, and current participants. It makes a difference to many young people that they will know a few of those already in the class.*

* Deal directly with the students, if possible. *Messages through parents, or pressure on parents, may not achieve the results you desire. Make an exception for action you seek from the parent.*

* Always keep an attitude of genuine concern. *Young people can tell whether you care about them or just about their attendance. Good attendance-building will always be people-building.*

FLEXIBILITY IS IMPORTANT

As with physical exercise, when leading a youth Bible study, it pays to stay flexible. Remember that you are teaching people, not just a lesson. The lesson could not be written for your class exactly as it will exist every time you meet—even if you were to write it yourself. You must keep your class's size, age, background, and knowledge in mind as you prepare a lesson. This does not imply any lack of worth in the materials. But it makes you, the Bible-study leader, a critical element in the lesson.

You are the composer, the arranger, the playmaker. You are the best judge of the likely response of your class to the suggested activities. And you are capable of making needed choices and adjustments or finding alternatives that will appeal to your students.

You are the one who is "on site" during the class. Circumstances may dictate last-minute adjustments or wholesale revisions of your lesson plan.

Flexibility abilities:

* *Choose lesson activities based on your knowledge of the class. (If the activities seem likely to be boring, they probably will be.)*

* *Keep an activity or two in mind or on hand for unexpected extra time or changes in plans. Successful activities from other lessons can be adapted. Books and magazines full of ideas are readily available.*

* *Respond to substantive concerns expressed in class. ("That's an important issue. Let's take some time to discuss it right now/at the end of class/next week.")*

* *Flexibility will impress your students, improve your studies, and help you stay sane.*

1

getting the best of them

LESSON FOCUS

Parent-teen relationships, when they reflect the model of Christ and the church, are a source of blessing for both parents and young people. Too often, however, their sinful nature obscures God's intentions and these relationships are full of competition and conflict.

GOSPEL FOCUS

Christ's forgiveness at work in parents and their teens will create a climate of forgiveness, acceptance, and cooperation.

Lesson Outline

ACTIVITY	SUGGESTED TIME	MATERIALS NEEDED
Family Feuds	10 minutes	None
A Little Respect	10 minutes	Copies of Student Page, Bibles
The First Family Fight	10 minutes	Copies of Student Page, Bibles
Think about It	10 minutes	Copies of Student Page, Bibles
Godly Qualities (optional)	15 minutes	Copies of Bonus Page, Bibles
Closing	5 minutes	None

A NOTE TO THE LEADER

Today families come in an array of combinations. Stepparents, single parents, live-in companions, joint-custody parents, and absentee parents are all part of the families of youth. Although this study is not intended to address any of the difficulties that are unique to these family situations, you will want to be sensitive in your terminology and assumptions.

FAMILY FEUDS (10 MINUTES)

This game illustrates the confusion that results from poor communication. Involve students in role-playing typical family "squabbles." In each case, appoint one or two "parents" and two "young people" to a family. Take the two "young people" aside. Tell them the situation, but invite them to make up additional details. Instruct one of them to always be completely honest. Tell the other to avoid telling the whole truth.

Sample situations

1. Two young people came home very late last night from a friend's house.

2. One youth has used another's favorite T-shirt to wash his or her car.

After a minute or two of preparation by the "young people," announce the basic conflict to the class and invite the "parent(s)" to initiate a problem-solving conversation with the "young people." The parents' goal is to get to the bottom of things as quickly as possible. Stop the action when things start to wind down or before things get out of hand.

After each situation, debrief with questions such as these: Was the role-play realistic? What would you have done or said differently if you were . . .? How did you feel when . . .? Was the problem difficult to solve? Why?

A LITTLE RESPECT (10 MINUTES)

Distribute copies of the Student Page to students in small groups and direct their attention to this section. It would seem easy enough to solve the problems that most parents and children have with one another. (We could easily use the word teens or youth here, but there are plenty of 40-year-old children who can't make a relationship with their parents work.) In Ephesians, Paul presents a foolproof way of getting along. Allow time for students to read the Bible passage and discuss the questions for about 5 minutes. Then invite volunteers to share their responses. Include the following in the discussion.

1. Ephesians 6:1–4 is a simple passage. Even if we didn't have a passage like this in the Bible, it is plain, common sense. God's plan is for people to love and respect one another. Most young people will already know this.

2. The answer, of course, is sin. Not just sin in the sense of a particular wrong-doing, but sin in the sense of the original corruption that infects our relationship with God and, as a consequence, every other relationship we have.

THE FIRST FAMILY FIGHT (10 MINUTES)

Allow students to work in small groups to read Genesis 3:6–13 and review the questions in this section. After about 8 minutes bring groups together to discuss their insights. In response to question 1, students may volunteer a variety of answers—sin, guilt, and rebellion. Accept all reasonable responses. Before the sin of disobedience committed by Adam and Eve, God never asked questions. After the fall, the first thing God did was to ask questions. Like Adam and Eve, our answers are always lies, half-truths, and evasions. Remember the game. When you don't know the whole truth, communication becomes impossible. Many family fights from Adam until now seem to follow this same pattern.

THINK ABOUT IT (10 MINUTES)

Direct the students to this section of the Student Page. Ephesians 2:11–18 distinguishes the effects of Law and Gospel. The Law always condemns. The Gospel always forgives. The Law always separates. The Gospel always unites. Look for words and phrases like "separate," "excluded," "foreigners," "far away," "barrier," and "dividing wall." Then look for words and phrases like "citizenship," "brought near," "making peace," and "reconcile." Emphasize that Christ's death on the cross destroyed the hostility that existed between God and people because of sin. Through Jesus' forgiveness God empowers us to forgive, to reconcile, and to make peace.

Christian families will not always reflect the relationship that they have with God because of Christ's work. But empowered by Jesus' love and forgiveness, it is possible to demonstrate love and forgiveness.

OPTIONAL ACTIVITY—GODLY QUALITIES (15 MINUTES)

Distribute copies of Bonus Page 1. Direct students, in small groups, to use their Bibles to complete the chart on this page. After about 10 minutes, invite groups to report on each passage and see if other groups agree or have additional responses. Answers may vary, but here are sample characteristics from each passage. Seek to emphasize these points in your discussion.

Colossians 1:21–23a—A relationship with Jesus changes a person from the enemy to one free from accusation. Having parents who share our faith is a blessing and gives us a common foundation.

Colossians 2:2–3—Encouragement, unity, understanding, wisdom, and knowledge. As Jesus offers these gifts to us, the Spirit working in us enables us to share them with others. These qualities are the base for strong communication in a family.

Colossians 2:6–7—Rooted and built up in Christ, strong in faith, thankful. These attitudes provide a strong base for building love and trust.

Colossians 3:8–10—Actively working with the Spirit to rid oneself of sinful action and being renewed in God's image. A person with this view is open to changing and desires a better way of living together with others.

Colossians 3:12–14—Compassion, kindness, humility, gentleness, patience, forgiveness, and love are given to us by God; we share them with others.

Colossians 3:20–21—Parents have been made authorities over their children to guide and protect them until they are able to take care of themselves. This relationship requires obedience from children and tender respect from parents.

Remind students that since these are qualities God desires in all His children, they can begin working on them in their lives now. People having these qualities will have richer, more satisfying relationships. Encourage teens to pray for their parents and their relationship.

CLOSING (5 MINUTES)

Say, "Although God's Word is not a family-life manual, it does illustrate God's love for us. As the Holy Spirit works through God's Word to strengthen our faith, we are able to demonstrate Jesus' love and forgiveness as we live through the dramas that occur in family relationships."

Close with a circle prayer. Invite students to offer one-sentence prayers for their parents and their family relationships. Let anyone who wishes simply say, "Lord, have mercy" or "Amen."

1. getting the best of them

a little respect

Read **Ephesians 6:1–4.**

1. If everyone followed Paul's instructions, what would families be like?

2. Why doesn't this happen in some families much of the time and in most families all of the time?

Sometimes just knowing the solution doesn't help the problem. But knowing where the problem comes from can be the key to solving the problem.

the first family fight

Read **Genesis 3:6–13**. Remember that God and His "children"—Adam and Eve—were very close to one another. God never once had to ask a question, pry, quiz, or otherwise dig around to find out what was going on or what His children were doing.

1. What words describe this "family fight?"

2. Do these same words describe "family fights" in your home?

think about it

Read **Ephesians 2:11–18.** Look for words and phrases that describe how people relate to one another in both positive and negative ways.

1. Give examples of times when your relationship with your parents reflected the sin that has infected us since Adam and Eve's fall.

2. Give examples of times when your relationship with your parents reflected the reconciliation God earned for us through Jesus' death on the cross.

3. What characteristics do you admire most in your parents or other parents?

bonus page 1

godly qualities

Read the selected verses from Colossians and identify the godly qualities for family members mentioned there.

Colossians	Godly Qualities for Family Members
1:21–23a	
2:2–3	
2:6–7	
3:8–10	
3:12–14	
3:20–21	

parents

surviving a split without coming apart

LESSON FOCUS

Divorce impacts the lives of young people. Statistics suggest that 33 percent of first marriages will end in divorce within 10 years (source: www.CDC.gov). Teens need a clear understanding of what God's Word teaches about divorce.

GOSPEL FOCUS

Some teens may carry a burden of guilt or an unfair sense of responsibility for the separation of their parents. They need to hear God's message of forgiveness through Jesus. Jesus' love empowers young people to forgive their parents for the hurts caused by divorce.

Lesson Outline

ACTIVITY	SUGGESTED TIME	MATERIALS NEEDED
Color Me . . .	5 minutes	Index cards, markers/crayons
Divorce Quiz	10 minutes	Copies of Student Page
Forgiving and Forgetting	15 minutes	Copies of Student Page, Bibles
Living with the Reality of Divorce	15 minutes	Copies of Student Page
Closing	5 minutes	None

COLOR ME . . . (5 MINUTES)

Give each student a note card and crayons or markers. Ask students to color the card with the colors that best seem to describe divorce and its effects. (They do not have to create a picture—only color the card.) Arrange the students in groups of three to five people. Direct them to share their names, show their card, and share the reason for their choice of colors. Avoid judgment of their choices.

Open with this prayer: "Dear Father, we know that You are with us in all things—through the hurt, the pain, and the joys of our lives. We ask that You be with us now as we discuss and seek to understand a very painful topic. We ask Your blessing on our study, and we pray for Your love to surround us and fill us. Make us sensitive to the needs of others and to Your will. In Jesus' name we ask this. Amen!"

Then say, "We are going to talk about divorce. We do not expect to solve all the problems surrounding this issue. We will share our feelings concerning the subject, see what God's Word has to say about divorce, find out what people experience when there is a divorce, and find ways to cope with our feelings and those of others when we or someone we care about experiences divorce."

DIVORCE QUIZ (10 MINUTES)

Hand out copies of the Student Page and ask students to respond to the true-or-false statements. Have someone read one or more of the suggested Bible references listed below. Have students compare their responses to God's expectations.

1. True—God intends married couples to stay together "until death parts us." An imperfect world creates imperfect marriages and imperfect solutions to problems (Matthew 5:31–32; Malachi 2:13–16).

2. False—Jesus does admit that His Father, through Moses, allowed divorce. It is clear that Jesus opposes divorce (Mark 10:1–9; Matthew 19:3–12).

3. False—Harboring a grudge in anger is sinful, just like divorce (Ephesians 4:31–32; Romans 2:1).

4. False—God forgives all sins confessed through faith in Jesus (1 John 1:9; 1 John 3:4–5).

FORGIVING AND FORGETTING (15 MINUTES)

Say, "The forgiveness Jesus won for us through His death at Calvary is totally complete and comprehensive. When God forgives our sins, He removes them 'as far as the east is from the west' (Psalm 103:12). That's a poetic way of saying He forgets all about them—period. He doesn't remind us of them over and over; He doesn't keep getting angry again and again. One problem with divorce is that, humanly speaking, it's difficult to forget how much we've been hurt."

Have students work in small groups to answer the questions on the Student Page. After seven or eight minutes, invite volunteers to share responses from their groups. The following comments can be emphasized:

1. *In order for us to have true peace with God and other people, we must be willing to forgive others.*

2. *By the power of the Holy Spirit, God enables us to forgive, because He has forgiven us. When we say, "Forgive us our trespasses as we forgive those who trespass against us," we ask God to forgive us as we forgive others.*

3. *Affirm student responses that focus on the Gospel at work in the lives of those whose faith and family relationships are strengthened by the Holy Spirit working through God's Word and Sacraments.*

LIVING WITH THE REALITY OF DIVORCE (15 MINUTES)

Assign each small group one of the situations on the Student Page. Or involve the entire class in the discussion of each situation as a large group. If students work in groups, allow time for each group to share its findings. Encourage students to be sensitive, thoughtful, and Gospel-centered as they discuss each situation. When discussing students' responses, stress God's abundant forgiveness and unending love.

CLOSING (5 MINUTES)

Pray, "Lord, we thank You for being with us in all things. We especially thank You for the blessings You have bestowed on us during this study. We thank You for the discussion, for the sharing, for the compassion. Please be with us now and in all things as we pray the prayer You taught us." (Speak the Lord's Prayer in unison.)

2. SURVIVING a SPLit Without coming apart

diVORCe QUiZ

Circle your responses to the following statements:

    T   F   1. Divorce is not a part of God's plan.

    T   F   2. In the New Testament Jesus says that divorce is okay.

    T   F   3. It's okay to stay angry with your parents if they divorce.

    T   F   4. Divorce is an unforgivable sin.

FORGiViNG aNd FORGettiNG

1. What does God say is necessary for us to live in peace with those who have hurt us (**Ephesians 4:31–32**)?

2. How are God's people able to forgive others (**Colossians 3:13**)?

3. Current studies reveal that an average of 33 percent of first marriages ends in divorce within 10 years. Experts indicate, however, that divorce rates are significantly reduced for those who have not lived together before marriage, who attend church regularly, and who participate in family worship activities.

How would you account for this difference?

LiViNG WiTH the ReaLiTY OF diVORCE

The following situations suggest some of the problems, fears, and decisions faced by individuals and families touched by divorce. Determine what issues need to be addressed in each case and how you could respond in a helpful, loving, and Christian manner.

1. Karen's parents probably think Karen can't hear them screaming at each other behind their closed bedroom door. But no room could contain the shouts that have become a regular fixture in Karen's home. Her mother accuses her dad of not really working all the many hours he is away from home. Her dad says he has no choice but to work to pay for all the things her mother keeps buying. Karen figures one day her dad will slam the door and never come back.

2. Zack and his brothers were shocked when their mom moved out. They hadn't heard any arguing, threats, crying, or anything else to give them a clue that their parents planned to end their marriage. Now their mom is gone, and their dad is begging the boys not to tell anyone that their mom has left. It is getting harder and harder to pretend that everything is okay, but Zack's father insists he can't handle all the gossip that will result when people find out what happened.

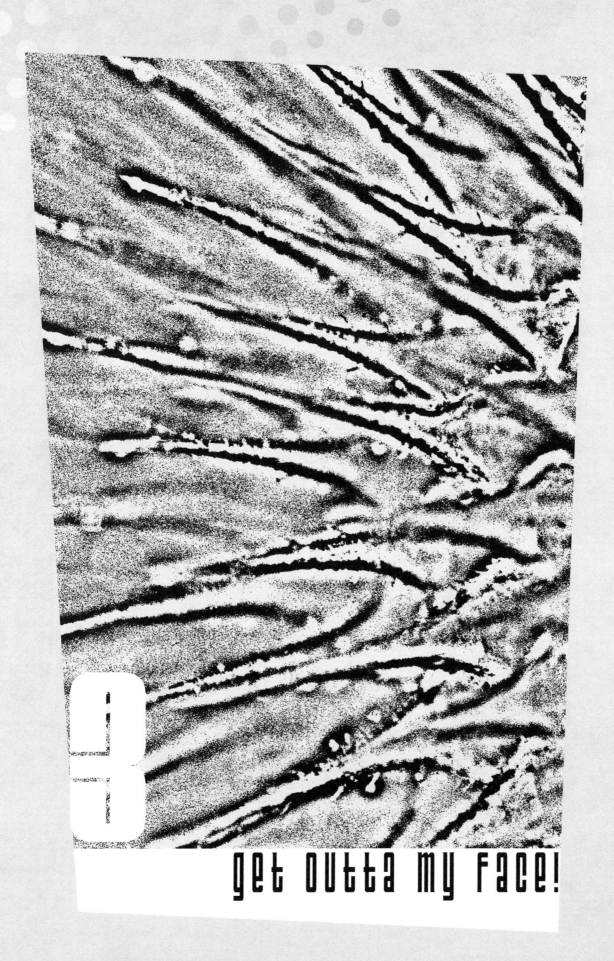

9

get outta my face!

LESSON FOCUS

Our sinful nature would deny our faults and sinful behavior. It prevents us from seeking forgiveness. It also leads us to see and criticize the faults and sins of others in our family and to ignore opportunities for reconciliation.

GOSPEL FOCUS

God in His grace has forgiven us through Christ. He offers us His strength to confront our sins and the sins of others. This Good News is at the core of the solution to conflict. Not through our efforts, but through Christ in us, we are empowered to strengthen our family relationships through forgiveness.

Lesson Outline

ACTIVITY	SUGGESTED TIME	MATERIALS NEEDED
What's Your Beef?	5 minutes	newsprint or board, index cards
The Shape of Things (optional)	5 minutes	construction paper and tape
Fight'n 'n' Feud'n	15 minutes	Copies of Student Page, Bibles
Families Forgive	10 minutes	Copies of Student Page
We Are Family!	15 minutes	Copies of Student Page
Sharing My Love	10 minutes	Copies of Student Page
Closing	5 minutes	None

WHAT'S YOUR BEEF? (5 MINUTES)

Draw a continuum on a sheet of newsprint. Include the following information: 1 = No problem at all; 2 = Sort of a problem; 3 = Really quite a problem; 4 = Terrific problem. Mount it on a bulletin board or the wall.

Give each student an index card. Have participants respond on the card with a number for each of the following situations (lettered A through D) to show how hard this would be for them.

Situation A: Forgiving a brother or sister who embarrassed you in front of your friends at school.

Situation B: Forgiving a parent who punished you unjustly.

Situation C: Forgiving a family member who put you down in front of your friends.

Situation D: Forgiving yourself when you have wronged a family member.

Allow time for discussion. When all have had a chance to complete the task, ask, "What makes it difficult to forgive family members?"

OPTIONAL OPENING—THE SHAPE OF THINGS (5 MINUTES)

Provide construction paper. Ask students to tear a sheet into the shape of an item they have fought about recently, add the name of the person with whom they fought, and tape it to their shirt. (For example, tear out a shape of a car and write "Mom" on it if the argument was with Mom about use of the family car.) Invite volunteers to explain their shape. Open the class session with prayer, asking for God's grace and strength in dealing with conflicts in a Christlike way.

FIGHT'N 'N' FEUD'N (15 MINUTES)

Direct students to this section on the Student Page. Ask someone to read Genesis 50:15–21. Ask, "What tension is obvious in the story?" (The brothers were afraid that Joseph would hate them or try to get even with them for their evil actions against him.)

Divide your class into small groups of three to five students and ask each group to skim or review the events in Genesis 37:1–34. Say, "Look for the reason the brothers feared Joseph." Ask each group to summarize the family history on the Student Page. Allow students to share their summaries.

Then ask, "What's the most striking part of this family story?" Invite several responses. Here are some possible answers:

* *Joseph's brothers ask for forgiveness.*

* *Joseph's father urges the brothers to ask for Joseph's forgiveness.*

* *The brothers send a messenger to ask for forgiveness from Joseph rather than going themselves.*

* *Joseph cries when he hears the messenger ask for forgiveness.*

* Joseph is able to forgive his brothers.

FAMILIES FORGIVE (10 MINUTES)

Have students work alone to rank the responses in this section. Then have students share their responses in small groups. After students have had time to share, say, "Now I'd like you to think of relationships within your own family."

WE ARE FAMILY! (15 MINUTES)

In a similar fashion, have students work independently to rank the important needs in their families. Give students time to share their rankings and the reasons for them in their small groups.

After students have finished this activity, share something along the following lines: "God's love for Joseph enabled him to forgive his brothers, in spite of the terrible things they had done to him. God in His love for us sent Jesus to receive the punishment we deserved because of our sin toward Him and others. We don't deserve God's love. Instead, purely out of His grace—undeserved love—God forgives us through our faith in Jesus. God's love and forgiveness enable us to love and forgive others. We live out God's love for us every time we forgive someone. With our faith strengthened through God's Word and His Sacraments, we are empowered by the Holy Spirit to show concern for our family's welfare. We can refuse to judge the behavior of our family members harshly or unjustly. We can confront wrongs by family members honestly and fairly. We can express our faith in Jesus with our family. And we can forgive members of our family when they have wronged us."

SHARING MY LOVE (10 MINUTES)

Direct the students to this section on the Student Page. Say, "I want you to think of each member of your family. Think of one person in your family who especially needs your love. Jot down a few words or phrases that describe how you might share love with this person." Allow time for volunteers to share.

CLOSING (5 MINUTES)

Close with a prayer. Focus on our gratitude for God's gift of family, forgiveness for all family members for the times when we fail one another and when we fail to live up to God's desire and purpose for families, our gratitude for the gift of forgiveness and the opportunity to share it with others, and help to love all members of our family.

3. get outta my face!

fight'n 'n' feud'n

Read **Genesis 50:15–21**. Then skim **Genesis 37:1–34** to determine the reason for the tension among family members. Summarize the family history:

families forgive

What was the most important message Joseph gave to his brothers?
(Rank in order of importance: 1=most important to 5=least important. Explain your reasoning.)

_____ a. "Don't be afraid."

_____ b. "Am I in the place of God?"

_____ c. "You intended to harm me."

_____ d. "But God intended it for good."

_____ e. "I will provide for you and your children."

family conflict

we are family!

What is the most important thing needed in your family: (Rank in order of importance: 1=most important to 5=least important. Explain your reasoning.)

_____ a. To show concern for my family's welfare.

_____ b. To refuse to judge unjustly or harshly the behavior of family members.

_____ c. To confront wrongs honestly and fairly.

_____ d. To express my faith in Jesus with my family.

_____ e. To forgive members of my family when they have wronged me.

sharing my love

One member of my family who especially needs my love is _____ _____.

I can demonstrate my love by _____.

not just a remote
social problem

LESSON FOCUS

Many people have been or may be victims of child abuse. Victims of child abuse need to know the love and forgiveness of God. They need the love and concern of their fellow Christians. We cannot begin to give them what they need until we get over our own awkwardness with the topic. The immorality of abuse and its unacceptability in our lives must be stressed. It is unlikely that the Law needs to be addressed to those who have experienced abuse as children, unless they have become abusers themselves.

GOSPEL FOCUS

God's grace and love should be extended to those involved in abuse in any way, although they may find it difficult to believe that God can love them. God forgives and renews all who repent and confess their sins, including the sin of the abuse of children. In fact, God's forgiveness is what leads them to confess and repent!

Lesson Outline

ACTIVITY	SUGGESTED TIME	MATERIALS NEEDED
What Is the Truth?	10 minutes	Chalkboard/chalk or newsprint/markers
Some Common Myths	10 minutes	Copies of Student Page
Hearing God's Law	10 minutes	Copies of Student Page, Bibles
Hearing Good News	15 minutes	Copies of Student Page, Bibles
An Emotional Issue	10 minutes	Copies of Student Page
Closing	5 minutes	None

AN IMPORTANT NOTE TO THE LEADER

As you prepare for this lesson, be aware of the potential that one or more of your students is, or may become, the victim of some form of abuse—including verbal, physical, and sexual abuse. Be sensitive as you plan your lesson and as you lead the discussion of this delicate topic. Familiarize yourself with the materials. Discussing the topic with another adult beforehand may help to ease any anxieties you may have.

WHAT IS THE TRUTH? (10 MINUTES)

Write the following questions on the chalkboard or on a large piece of paper. Display them in a prominent location.

True or False?

1. As many as one out of every four people is abused before the age of 18.

2. Boys are seldom abused.

3. Children are usually abused by strangers they meet on the street.

Have students read the true-or-false statements and record on a piece of scrap paper what they believe the correct answers to be. Or let them vote either true or false on newsprint or the chalkboard, using either marker, sticky dots, or chalk. Ask them to watch for evidence confirming or refuting their choices throughout the session.

Spend some time discussing students' preconceptions of what a child abuser looks like. What do students imagine when they hear "child abuser"? What does he or she look like? How does he or she act? Is the abuser male or female? How is he or she dressed? Would you easily recognize a child abuser in a crowd of people? Why do people often picture child abusers in this way?

SOME COMMON MYTHS (10 MINUTES)

Read or have students read each of the myths on the Student Page. After each is read, discuss it as a group.

1. Child abuse does not happen often. *Research indicates that as many as one out of every three or four girls, and one out of every 10 boys, is a victim of sexual abuse as a child or adolescent. The number of abused and neglected children has increased anywhere from 107 to 188 percent in the past 10 years (source: U.S. Department of Health and Human Services at www.hhs.gov). Consider how these statistics translate into real people if applied to your local high school.*

2. Child sexual abuse occurs only when a child is inappropriately touched on a private part of his or her body. *Child sexual abuse usually includes touching, but not always. Anything that has a negative effect upon a child's sense of sexuality is abusive. It can include physical contact up to and including rape, but it also includes peeping, using sexually explicit language, and forcing a child to look at pornographic materials.*

3. Child abuse happens only in economically poor areas. *Abuse and abusers are found among all economic, social, and ethnic groups. Just as the sin of lying exists at all levels of humanity, so does the sin of abuse.*

4. Child abusers are strangers. They are generally older, unkempt individuals who wear trench coats. Most abused children, (85–90 percent) are abused by someone they know—most often a relative. Child abusers have no physical similarities drawing attention to the sin in which they are involved. They can and do look like everyone else.

HEARING GOD'S LAW (10 MINUTES)

Read or have volunteers read Leviticus 18:1–6, 29–30. Form the class into three or more groups if possible. Strive for four to seven people in each group. Direct the groups to discuss the questions about these verses found on the Student Page. After about seven minutes, invite volunteers to share their group's responses to each question. The following points should be made in discussion:

1. "I am the LORD your God" is repeated four times in these verses. Why is this reminder important to you? (We are creatures of a powerful God. He is able to punish. He is also able to keep the promises He makes to save His people.)

2. Why did God give these laws (and many others) to His people in the wilderness? (God gave His laws as a form of protection for Israel, to preserve them during the wilderness wandering and the conquest of Canaan.)

3. In what ways do contemporary Christians live "in the wilderness"? (We have pressures toward living like "pagans"—people without God. Our disobedience to God's commands still results in spiritual and eternal death unless we are rescued through Christ.)

HEARING GOOD NEWS (15 MINUTES)

Read or have someone else read Ephesians 2:1–10. Assign each small group one of the perspectives from the Student Page. Direct them to review and discuss the passage from that perspective (such as the perspective of one who has been abused), addressing the following questions. (You may find it helpful to write these on newsprint or the chalkboard.)

 * *What hope does Paul offer for that person?*

 * *What does the future hold for that person?*

 * *What actions might that person's faith in Christ prompt him or her to do?*
 After about 10 minutes, again allow volunteers from each group to share.

AN EMOTIONAL ISSUE (10 MINUTES)

Have students react to the questions on the Student Page. The following comments may be helpful during discussion:

1. Victims of abuse experience many varied emotions. What might some of them be? (Some of the possible emotions the students may choose are anger at losing the innocence of childhood at an early age; fear of the possibility of the abuse continuing or happening again; depression because of the losses endured; loneliness because of the feeling of not being able to tell someone about the pain; or guilt over feeling responsible for what happened.)

2. How might they deal with or cope with each of these emotions? (People express their emotions in many different ways. For example, a person struggling to cope with the burden of abuse may become very quiet or perhaps very boisterous.)

3. What are the needs of victims of abuse? (Victims of abuse have to take their shattered lives and begin to rebuild them. They have to leave behind their lives as victims, where the abuser has a sort of control over them and where they are fearful much of the time. And they have to become survivors. They need confidence in the strength that is theirs through Jesus Christ. They must learn that they can do all things through Him, firm in the faith that nothing can separate them from the love of God. By the power of the forgiveness He has provided through His life, death, and resurrection, they can forgive the person who victimized them. As the Holy Spirit works peace, joy, and strength through the means of grace, the person who has been abused can travel the long, difficult road to recovery.)

4. How can you help persons who have been the victims of abuse as you share the love of Jesus with them? (Help the students to evaluate the suggestions given about ways to care for others. Listening to, supporting, praying for, and standing up for the abused are all ways to help.)

Note: Question 4 presents a good opportunity to remind your students that if they are being abused, or if they suspect that someone else is being abused, they should tell a teacher, their pastor, or another trusted adult. Stress that help is available and that silence all too often keeps the cycle of abuse going. (You might also find the phone numbers of local abuse prevention organizations and make this information available to your students.)

CLOSING (5 MINUTES)

Mention that people are often reluctant to talk about this topic, but that talking about child abuse will help to raise awareness and understanding of it. Think about what you would do if a friend told you he or she had been or is being abused. Pray for the sufferers of abuse. Pray also for the abusers, that they would see the grace and love of the Lord and turn from their ways.

Close with this prayer: "Dear Father in heaven, we look around this world that You once created perfect, and we see imperfection. Many people are hurting and suffering because of the sin that exists. Keep us mindful of the grace that You showed all of us when Jesus suffered on the cross and of the glory He experienced in His rising from the grave—the glory that will one day be ours in heaven. In Jesus' name we pray. Amen."

4. not Just a Remote Social Problem

Some Common Myths

1. Child abuse does not happen often.

2. Child sexual abuse occurs only when a child is inappropriately touched on a private part of his or her body.

3. Child abuse happens only in economically poor areas.

4. Child abusers are strangers. They are generally older, unkempt individuals who wear trench coats.

Hearing God's Law

*Read **Leviticus 18:1–6, 29–30**. Respond to the following questions:*

1. "I am the LORD your God" is repeated four times in these verses. Why is this reminder important to you?

2. Why did God give these laws (and many others) to His people in the wilderness?

3. In what ways do contemporary Christians live "in the wilderness"?

Hearing Good News

*Read **Ephesians 2:1–10**. Consider this passage from three perspectives. What hope is present and what future actions are possible for these people?*

Someone who has been abused as a child

Someone who has abused others

You

An Emotional Issue

1. Victims of abuse experience many varied emotions. What might some of them be?

2. How might they deal with or cope with each of these emotions?

3. What are the needs of victims of abuse?

4. How can you help persons who have been the victims of abuse as you share the love of Jesus with them?

5

making the recipe work

LESSON FOCUS

Divorce and remarriage touch the lives of countless teens. During adolescence, when family relationships are already frequently strained, it is an additional challenge to deal with emotions left over from a parent's divorce or death and relate in healthy ways to stepparents and stepsiblings. With God's help, young people can confess sinful attitudes toward their parents and siblings in these blended families. They can discover healthy ways to communicate their feelings and make the blended family work.

GOSPEL FOCUS

We can assure teens affected by the loss of a parent that their sinful attitudes are forgiven through faith in Jesus as God and that He leads them to repentance. God works through His Word and the Sacraments to change resentment to respect and even love.

Lesson Outline

ACTIVITY	SUGGESTED TIME	MATERIALS NEEDED
Opening	10 minutes	None
Lights, Camera, Action	10 minutes	Copies of script, video equipment
The Premier	15 minutes	Copies of Student Page, TV/VCR, newsprint
Forgiveness Power	10 minutes	Copies of Student Page, Bibles, newsprint
Closing	5 minutes	None

A NOTE TO THE LEADER

This lesson can be enriched through the use of a video camera and monitor, on which to show the final result. Most teens are very proficient in the operation of such equipment. If you do not have a camera of your own, see if you can borrow one.

Obtain, set up, and test the equipment well ahead of class. Consider meeting in a location that will lend itself to the presentation and recording of the skit. If your group is large, consider dividing into two or more "production crews," each with its own cast and camera.

OPENING (10 MINUTES)

Greet each student upon arrival. Recruit students to take the parts in the skit. Others could be recruited for recording, preparing the set (a few chairs in a semi-circle), or helping the "players" rehearse. Allow a few extra minutes for preparation before beginning class.

Then lead an opening prayer of thanksgiving for families and asking for help in family relationships.

LIGHTS, CAMERA, ACTION (15 MINUTES)

Distribute copies of the script as needed. Allow students time to review the script and rehearse. Help the students enjoy themselves. Involve students without parts in analyzing the lines ("_____, how would you have said that line? Does that sound realistic to you?") Remind the group that they will soon be taped. All in all, make it a time of joyful learning of the themes in the Bible text.

Don't expect students to memorize their lines. And don't worry about perfection. When the rehearsal time is up, encourage the players to do their best, and "roll the cameras." Videotape the skit. An occasional "retake" can be allowed, but don't use all of your time trying to get things perfect.

THE PREMIER (20 MINUTES)

Provide copies of the Student Page. As students watch the tape, have them take notes about things that made them laugh, think, or question. Begin by asking the students what really hit them during the skit. Did a certain character, comment, or Scripture verse catch their attention?

Direct the students into small groups of three to five. Give them 10 minutes to discuss the questions. Then invite groups to share their responses to each question. Use the comments after each question to assist your discussion.

1. Does the attitude of Player 1 at the beginning say anything about his/her family life? (Player 1 seems to show a disrespect of authority. It is a common biblical theme throughout Holy Scripture to show respect for authority—even to the Roman Empire, as explained in Romans 13:1–7.)

2. *Why do you think God chose parents to create and raise you? (Emphasize that God created us through our biological parents. We may not always understand His reasons or our parents' actions, however. God also may use the parents of others to nurture us in life. In either case, it is according to His will.)*

3. *Why is it sometimes hard to obey your parents? (Discuss the fall into sin in Genesis 3 and its impact on human nature. When God tells a person not to do something—that person's natural response is to do it. Also point out the different traditions and rules that are learned in families. In blended families, these traditions may cause confusion and conflict.)*

4. *How much do you honor or value your parents? How does this reflect in your actions toward them? (Discuss the attitudes students have about their parents.)*

5. *Player 3 seemed upset and didn't want to live a long life. Can you tell what the problem is from the skit? (We have a natural tendency to exaggerate our difficulties in life. This can lead to negative attitudes. This may be the case for Player 3, or the person may be living in a troubled family. Either way, God cares about us. He desires that we care for one another.)*

6. *How do we find relief from our sinful attitudes toward others? (We know that Jesus died for every person in the world, so that by grace, through faith, all can receive eternal life. This reality helps us to see people in a much different way. As God loves me and others, so I can love others.)*

7. *What can we do to forgive and heal the wounds in family strife? (Help the group discover practical tools for improving family relationships, such as communication without defensiveness, honorable attitudes, praying for hurtful people, talking with other Christians to get advice. These could be written on newsprint or the board for all to see and absorb.)*

FORGIVENESS POWER

Invite someone to read Colossians 2:13–15 out loud. Direct the students to respond to the questions in small groups. After a few minutes, invite each group to respond to one of the questions. Incorporate the following comments into the discussion:

1. *Who is involved in the relationship? (The passage talks about the relationship between God and people re-established through the person and work of Jesus.)*

2. Describe the relationship before the forgiveness offered through Jesus. (There is no relationship at all; it is dead.)

3. Why was the relationship dead? (Our sinful human nature separates us from God.)

4. How was it restored? (Through Jesus' death God forgave us, canceled the note, and made us alive! He knows that it is not healthy for us to live in an unforgiven state, and so with His own life He forgives us.)

Now we are called to forgive and love as Christ has forgiven and loves us (Matthew 19:19; Mark 12:28–34; Luke 10:27; Romans 13:9). Such love—obedience to the Law—is not the result of our effort, but of the power of Christ at work in us.

On the board or on newsprint write the heading "Words and Actions That Show Forgiveness." Invite the class to brainstorm responses that fit the heading. Some will be general in nature; others will be specific to certain situations.

Invite students to turn to Colossians 2:13–15 again. Then say, "As you hear these words again, picture the joy of new life of forgiveness. Hear God's words of forgiveness for you and know that God in Christ Jesus does indeed love and forgive you." Read the passage to the class.

Then say, "Identify one person in your family to whom you need to speak a word of forgiveness. What actions or words could you use to reach out to that person? Make plans to speak those words or do those actions this week. Write a note to yourself on the back of the Student Page, describing what you intend to do."

CLOSING (5 MINUTES)

Invite a volunteer to close with prayer. Or lead a prayer yourself, thanking God for the forgiveness we receive through Jesus Christ and the Spirit's help as we begin to rebuild family relationships.

making the recipe work

blended families

5 making the recipe work——script

Pastor: We're studying **Ephesians 6:1–4**. Please turn to that passage.

Player 1: Boring. Bring out the pillows.

Player 2: How rude can someone be?

Pastor: It won't be boring. This passage of the Bible is relevant to your lives.

Player 1: Yeah, I bet.

Pastor: Why don't you read **verse 1**?

Player 1: *(Sighs)* "Children, obey your parents in the Lord, for this is right." Great.

Player 3: I really don't like being called a child. I'm an adult.

Pastor: The word *children* means "one born of." It emphasizes the fact that God created you through your parents.

Player 2: But my dad doesn't live with us. Should I obey him or my stepdad?

Pastor: You should obey both.

Player 2: Yeah, but what if they contradict each other?

Pastor: You should do your best to obey both.

Player 3: I sure don't like that word *obey*. Sounds like we're dogs or something.

Pastor: *Obey* means "to hear under." God has given you parents to guide you.

Player 3: But what if they are wrong?

Pastor: We have to examine right and wrong through the Word of God.

Player 2: My dad doesn't go to church, but my stepdad does.

Pastor: Read **verses 2 and 3**.

Player 2: " 'Honor your father and mother'—which is the first commandment with a promise— 'that it may go well with you and that you

may enjoy long life on the earth.' " So you live long if you obey your parents?

Player 1: Yeah, they don't kill you!

Pastor: The word *honor* also means "to value." I didn't realize how wonderful my parents were until my wife and I had a child. It is hard work.

Player 3: I don't know if I even want to live a long time. My family is messed up.

Pastor: The verse doesn't talk only about living a long time. It talks about obedience and honor—and things in life going well. Not perfect.

Player 1: I don't think it's that simple.

Pastor: The Bible doesn't promise that it will be easy. There are struggles.

Player 2: Hey! Look at the next verse! "Fathers, do not exasperate your children; instead, bring them up in the training and instruction of the Lord."

Player 3: So if we have to obey our parents, they at least have to work with us.

Pastor: Communication and loving relationships are the key. It reminds me of some of the words in the Lord's Prayer: "Forgive us our trespasses as we forgive those who trespass against us."

Player 2: It's sort of like trespassing that needs forgiveness—getting in each other's way.

Pastor: God loves us so much that He sent His only Son to die for our sins so that by grace, through faith, we may have eternal life. For Him, we then live to forgive and heal the many sins and wounds within the family.

Scripture quotations: NIV®. Used by permission of Zondervan.

39

5 MAKING THE RECIPE WORK——STUDENT PAGE

THE PREMIER

1. Does the attitude of Player 1 at the beginning say anything about his/her family life?

2. Why do you think God chose parents to create and raise you?

3. Why is it sometimes hard to obey your parents?

4. How much do you honor or value your parents?

   How does this reflect in your actions toward them?

5. Player 3 seemed upset and didn't want to live a long life. Can you tell what the problem is from the skit?

6. How do we find relief from our sinful attitudes toward others?

7. What can we do to forgive and heal the wounds in family strife?

blended families

FORGIVENESS POWER

*Read **Colossians 2:13–15.** It describes a relationship built upon and strengthened through forgiveness.*

1. Who is involved in the relationship?

2. Describe the relationship before the forgiveness offered through Jesus.

3. Why was the relationship dead?

4. How was it restored?

6

good grief?

LESSON FOCUS

Since the fall into sin, death remains a cruel and inescapable reality. Christians believe in the resurrection, yet they grieve when a friend or loved one dies. Some believe teens' lives are carefree and free from grief or pain. Through God's Word students are able to recognize God's hand in the events of life, especially as they experience trials. Grief and pain are not always the direct result of our sinful actions, though they are a result of sin in the world since the fall. We sin when we lose sight of God and His promises in the face of loss and turn away from Him.

GOSPEL FOCUS

God forgives us for Jesus' sake and promises His constant support and love, especially in difficult times. The Holy Spirit works in us the ability to walk by faith rather than sight. We look to Jesus for comfort, as did Mary and Martha at the death of Lazarus; He strengthens us to endure the pain, grow in faith, and face death with hope.

Lesson Outline

ACTIVITY	SUGGESTED TIME	MATERIALS NEEDED
Death: The Last Enemy?	10 minutes	Index cards or newsprint and markers, copies of Student Page
True or False	10 minutes	Copies of Student Page, Bibles
Dearly Departed	15 minutes	Bibles
Words of Comfort	15 minutes	Copies of Student Page, Bibles
Closing	10 minutes	Index cards, hymnals

A NOTE TO THE LEADER

Be aware of students who may have recently experienced the loss of a loved one or close friend. For additional ideas on how to support someone experiencing loss, see

What to Say: 52 Positive Ways to Show Christian Sympathy to Those Who Grieve by Carol Fredericks Ebeling, © 2002 Concordia Publishing House (item no. 12-4118).

DEATH: THE LAST ENEMY? (10 MINUTES)

Give each student an index card. Ask students to complete the phrase "Death is . . ." Urge them to consider more than one way to complete the phrase. Collect the cards and discuss their responses.

Or . . .

Write "Death is . . ." on the board or newsprint. Provide markers and urge students to complete the phrase. Give students time to discuss their responses. Accept all responses.

Say, "Many people say that death is the last enemy. Does this statement provide an accurate description of grief?" Urge students in groups of three to five to share personal experiences that support the description. Then have the small groups discuss the printed questions in this section on the Student Page.

Pray aloud the following: "Father, the death of a loved one can be so painful. As we study Your Word this day, help us discover Your healing power for our hurts and words of encouragement for those who are hurting. We pray in the name of our Lord Jesus, who conquered death and its sting through His death and resurrection. Amen."

TRUE OR FALSE (10 MINUTES)

Have students mark the statements on the Student Page concerning death and grief and share them with their small group. Bring them together to discuss their responses and the points below. After each statement is discussed, you may read or have a student read the appropriate Bible references.

a. John 11:35—When a Christian dies, we rejoice that through death they have received Christ's victory, but we also miss the dead person.

b. 1 Thessalonians 4:13—Believers' mourning or grief is tempered by hope in the victory Jesus proclaimed over death.

c. John 11:35—A person's ability to hold in feelings doesn't indicate strength. Jesus wept over the death of Lazarus.

d. John 11:32—In a moment we will see Jesus deal gently with the anger of Mary and Martha by reminding them of the promise of eternal life for all who believe in Him.

e. Matthew 5:4—There is no predetermined time for grief. Sobbing and inactivity eventually give way to less visible grieving.

DEARLY DEPARTED (15 MINUTES)

Have volunteers read John 11:17–45 aloud. Then discuss the following questions with the group as a whole:

What words of encouragement does Jesus provide to Martha (John 11:23)? ("Your brother will rise again.")

Why do you think pastors often use the words of Jesus in John 11:25–26 at funerals? (They offer a strong affirmation of eternal life.)

How does Jesus respond to Mary's grief (John 11:33–35)? (He grieves with her. Note that Jesus provides comfort to Mary and Martha without judging or denying their grief.)

How do Jesus' tears comfort us when we experience the death of a friend or relative? (He is not indifferent. He cares for us too.)

How does Jesus' raising Lazarus from the dead comfort us as we mourn? (It demonstrates His power to do the same for us.)

WORDS OF COMFORT (10 MINUTES)

Allow students to work together in small groups to complete this section. Assign each group one or more of the passages found on the Student Page. Ask groups to share how they might use this verse to comfort someone who is experiencing loss.

God has made us His own through our faith in Jesus. He comforts us in all trouble. Read 2 Corinthians 1:3–4 aloud. Ask, "What does God empower us to do with the comfort we receive from Him? From whom does the only real comfort come?"

CLOSING (10 MINUTES)

Give students another index card with the words "Death is . . ." printed on it. Have students complete the phrase again. Ask, "Has your attitude toward death and grief changed since the beginning of this session? If so, how?" Close with prayer.

6. good grief?

death: the last enemy?

1. What do you say to people who grieve?

2. Do you think grief over the death of a loved one can ever really die? Why or why not?

3. What do you think? Do people who grieve ever laugh again? Explain your answer.

true or false

* The death of a Christian is a happy occasion. **(John 11:35)**

* If your faith is strong enough, you won't grieve. **(1 Thessalonians 4:13)**

* If your faith is strong, you will hold in your feelings. **(John 11:35)**

* Anger during grief is unhealthy and un-Christian. **(John 11:32)**

* Grief is okay, but the process should stop after a week or so. **(Matthew 5:4)**

dearly departed

Read **John 11:17–45.**

What words of encouragement does Jesus provide to Martha **(John 11:23)**?

Why do you think pastors often use the words of Jesus in **John 11:25–26** at funerals?

How does Jesus respond to Mary's grief **(John 11:33–35)**?

How do Jesus' tears comfort us when we experience the death of a friend or relative?

How does Jesus' raising Lazarus from the dead comfort us as we mourn?

WORDS OF COMFORT

What messages of comfort are found in these verses?

Job 19:21–27

Psalms 23; 39; 46; 90; 121; 130; 139

Isaiah 25:6–9; 61:1–3

Lamentations 3:22–33

Matthew 28:20

John 5:24; 6:37–40; 10:27–29; 14:1–6

Romans 6:3–5; 8:31–39

1 Corinthians 15:1–26, 35–57

1 Thessalonians 4:13–18

1 Peter 1:3–9

1 John 3:1–2

Revelation 7:9–17; 21:2–7

7

addicted to helping

LESSON FOCUS

Co-dependents deny, cover up, and ignore the unhealthy behavior of others, thereby enabling them to stay unhealthy. All kinds of helping can be overdone—helping someone too much with homework so that they do not learn; being someone's closest and only friend so that they do not develop other relationships; covering for someone's drinking or substance abuse so that they do not face consequences. Young people will benefit from learning to recognize co-dependent behavior and to differentiate it from real service to others.

GOSPEL FOCUS

We respond to Jesus, who became a servant to us through His death on the cross, as we serve Him and others.

Lesson Outline

ACTIVITY	SUGGESTED TIME	MATERIALS NEEDED
Have You Ever?	15 minutes	Copies of Student Page
Think about It	15 minutes	Copies of Student Page
Words to Serve By	20 minutes	Bibles
Closing	5 minutes	None

A NOTE TO THE LEADER

Co-dependency is not a universally understood word. It means many things to many different people. For that reason many professionals have stopped using the word. But in popular culture, the word has come to describe a person who has poor boundaries. The co-dependent person doesn't know when to quit serving, doesn't know when to take a stand and confront an unhealthy behavior. By their service co-dependents enable others to commit unhealthy behavior.

The word co-dependent was used originally in the 1970s to describe the spouse of an alcoholic. The spouse would help the alcoholic cover up and deny the problem. He or she would work so that the alcoholic would never have to face the consequences of drinking. Originally, professionals thought the alcoholic relationship "caused" the co-dependency. But as they studied that personality type, they realized that most of those people came into the relationships with those same characteristics. People with co-dependent traits attract those with tendencies for substance abuse.

Christians have the call to serve above all else. It is helpful to be able to distinguish between the healthy service God desires and the co-dependent service that we frequently offer.

HAVE YOU EVER? (15 MINUTES)

Distribute copies of the Student Page. Divide the class into groups of three to five students. Direct the groups to share responses to the "Have You Ever?" questions. Give them plenty of time to tell their specific stories. These are designed to help them see that service can go bad. That is not God's idea. After the small groups have had a chance to share, invite responses to each question from the whole group. As you discuss, make the following point: "God does not desire that we serve until we are burned out and emotionally crippled. An important truth about servanthood is that we do not serve as people want to be served—we serve as God wants them to be served. What dysfunctional people think they need and what God desires them to have may be very different. We serve only as God motivates us through His love in Christ."

THINK ABOUT IT (15 MINUTES)

The discussion questions are meant to help the students define God-pleasing service—making distinctions between what God calls us to do and what others frequently want us to do.

Have the students rank each statement individually. Then invite them to share their responses in their small groups. As they discuss, challenge each group to improve statements with which they do not strongly agree by rewriting them. For example, the first statement could be strengthened by adding the words "as God desires them to be served." After about 10 minutes, invite the groups to share their corrected statements. The following are sample corrections of the statements. The ones your students prepare may be different, but valid.

* We should serve other people with 100 percent of our being, 100 percent of the time, as God desires them to be served.

* *It is* sometimes *wrong to get involved in other people's affairs.*

* *We should serve others as long as it doesn't infringe on our health and comfort.* (Some occasions of service may involve risk. Many will occur in uncomfortable circumstances. God does not require each of us to be martyrs, however.)

* Though serving others is sometimes difficult, *God always gives us the power to serve.*

* *Helping to the point of enabling unhealthy behavior* and not helping at all are both sinful.

* *Sharing the Gospel is the most important thing a Christian can do.* (Serving others is a close second: "Love the Lord your God with all your heart . . . love your neighbor as yourself" [Mark 12:30–31].)

WORDS TO SERVE BY (20 MINUTES)

Give each small group one of the following Bible passages. Direct them to discover what their passage has to say about God-pleasing service. After a few minutes ask each group to report. The comments after each verse will help the group evaluate each passage.

Amos 5:21–24: God is not pleased with token offerings when our heart is not in them. Only through faith, and empowered by Christ, can we serve God in a pleasing way.

Matthew 25:34–40: Our service to others is, in fact, service to God Himself. It can be so natural that we do not even realize that we have served.

Mark 10:35–45: Our service is never for the purpose of gaining honor or glory for ourselves. Christ sacrificed Himself for others to the point of death to pay for our sins. We cannot do that.

Luke 10:38–42: Service can never take the place of the nurture we receive through Word and Sacrament. These are the source of power for service.

After the reports, ask the students individually to write a summary of servanthood that is biblical and reflective of new understandings about co-dependency. On the back of the Student Page ask them to summarize healthy, biblical service by completing this statement—"Right now, God calls me to serve ..."—with three phrases answering the questions Whom? How? and When?" Encourage students to make a specific commitment to serve someone better or to stop enabling someone whom they are not really serving. If you know your class well, invite volunteers to share their commitment statements. Remind students that God motivates them to serve by His love revealed for them in the life, death, and resurrection of Jesus.

CLOSING (5 MINUTES)

Close by praying for the students. Ask that God will strengthen them to follow through on the commitments they have made. Give thanks for a better understanding of healthy servanthood.

7. addicted to helping

have you ever?

* Helped someone to the point where it ended up exhausting and debilitating you?

* Looked the other way when a friend was engaged in unhealthy behavior, not doing anything about it because it's your "friend"?

* Helped someone else, and it somehow backfired in your face?

* Gotten involved in relationship problems between two other people and become their "go-between"?

* Wondered how to best help someone in need?

think about it

Rate the following statements according to the following scale: 1=strongly agree; 2=agree; 3=not sure; 4=disagree; 5=strongly disagree. Be prepared to discuss your reasons.

_____ We should serve other people with 100 percent of our being, 100 percent of the time.

_____ It is always wrong to get involved in other people's affairs.

_____ We should serve others as long as it doesn't infringe on our health and comfort.

_____ There is nothing difficult about serving others, because God always gives us the power to serve.

_____ Helping to the point of enabling unhealthy behavior is less of a sin than not helping at all.

_____ Serving others is the most important thing a Christian can do.

words to serve by

What do these verses say about service?

Amos 5:21–24

Matthew 25:34–40

Mark 10:35–45

Luke 10:38–42

Right now, God calls me to serve . . .

8

"i'd date him/her, but . . ."

LESSON FOCUS

Young people may not automatically connect the growing attractions they feel for persons of the opposite sex with God's plan for marriage and family. The values and standards they apply to their dating and friendships may not, therefore, be those they would use in choosing a permanent partner. Understanding God's truths about dating can, therefore, bring new purpose, value, and joy to the developing social life of teens.

GOSPEL FOCUS

God desires couples to live in a permanent, one-flesh union. God's Word provides the standard by which we conduct ourselves socially. Through Christ we receive forgiveness for the times we fail to live up to those standards. The Holy Spirit strengthens us through the Word and Sacraments to live out the standard set for us in God's Word.

Lesson Outline

ACTIVITY	SUGGESTED TIME	MATERIALS NEEDED
Introduction	15 minutes	Magazines
My Ideal Date	10 minutes	Copies of Student Page
Looking at Marriage	15 minutes	Copies of Student Page, Bibles
Looking Ahead	15 minutes	Copies of Student Page, Bibles
Closing	5 minutes	None

A NOTE TO THE LEADER

Dating is a major issue for most young people. Unfortunately, the world has negatively impacted young people's understanding of appropriate dating behavior. If your students have additional questions about dating and sexuality, these resources may be helpful:

Guy Stuff/Girl Stuff: Dating and Sexuality by Tim and Melinda Walz (CPH item no. 20-3272). A four-session Bible study designed for single-gender groups.

The Why Files: When Can I Start Dating? by James N. Watkins (CPH item no. 12-4059). A book filled with students' questions, with answers from experts.

INTRODUCTION (15 MINUTES)

Direct students' attention to magazine articles you have gathered. (Check teen and fashion magazines, such as *YM, Seventeen, Cosmopolitan, Details, Spin,* and magazines available from Christian bookstores, such as *Break Away* for guys and *Brio* for girls.) Post stories, ads, and so forth on the walls or bulletin boards around the room or give them to students to read and pass along. Informally discuss the pictures, ads, stories, and such with students. Ask, "What messages about dating do you get?" Contrast *Brio* and *Break Away* advertising and visual images with the secular periodicals. List some responses on the board or newsprint.

Begin the study by saying, "One thing that's a vital part of your world is dating. Today I want to help you think about your dating experience or knowledge, look at what you want in a person you date, and get some solid input from Scripture about love, marriage, and your lives as dating Christians."

"I'd like to begin by asking you to think about the people you know at school, in your neighborhood, and here at church. No names now! How many of you know people who have had a positive experience with dating? If you do, just raise your hand. How many of you know people who have had a really bad experience with dating? Again, let me see a show of hands. How many of you know people who have decided not to date? Let me see a show of hands. What are some of the reasons people decide not to date?" (Could be busy with sports or academics, parents may say no, or negative experiences.)

After a few students have shared, pray for God's Spirit to guide your study of His Word as people discuss a very personal part of their life. Ask God to strengthen each person with His Word to better understand marriage and what it means to be truly prepared to marry.

MY IDEAL DATE (10 MINUTES)

Distribute copies of the Student Page and direct students to "My Ideal Date." Instruct them to pick their top five choices from each list. Give them a minute or two to make their choices. Have them share their choices with a partner. After four or five minutes ask for volunteers to share with the entire class. Be sure not to judge choices or comment, other than to express appreciation for their willingness to share.

LOOKING AT MARRIAGE (15 MINUTES)

Introduce the next section by saying, "To talk about dating, you really need to talk about marriage. Especially for us as Christians, it's important to talk about God's view of marriage. It's critical that we talk about His expectations for the way men and women live, love, and share life together."

Read, or have a volunteer read, Ephesians 5:22–28. Then say, "There are two key phrases in that text. They are listed on the Student Page." (Read the first one.) "In the space below that phrase, take a moment to write one or two things concerning what this phrase means for wives." Give them a moment to write; then read the second phrase and ask them to write one or two things concerning what this means for husbands. After they finish, ask for volunteers to share their responses.

Be affirming wherever possible. "God compares marriage to the relationship between Christ and the church. Wives are to submit as we submit to our Lord Himself, following His Word, affirming His forgiveness and love. A husband should love his wife as Christ loved the church." Remind the students that Christ loved so much that He willingly suffered and died on the cross for us while we were still sinners.

LOOKING AHEAD (15 MINUTES)

Introduce the closing sections something like this: "So the question really before us is, what does God's view of marriage really mean for us as we date, fall in love, build relationships of love and affection, and someday, for many, marry. Open your Bibles to 1 Corinthians 6:13–20." Ask a volunteer to read aloud as participants follow in their own Bibles. Then ask students to write on the Student Page one or two things this text has to say about dating and forming relationships. After giving them a minute or two to write, ask them to share with one person in the group. After about five minutes, invite volunteers to share their responses with the whole group.

Next read aloud, or have a volunteer read aloud, 1 Corinthians 13:4–13. Then ask each person to write the characteristics from this text that they would appreciate in a date or eventually a mate. Ask volunteers to share responses. Summarize the major things shared in class.

CLOSING (5 MINUTES)

Close with prayer. The prayer should thank God for the gift of relationships and for the models of responsible Christian love and marriage we have in Scripture, praise Him for the forgiveness He offers to repentant sinners for the times when they act or think contrary to God's will, and ask His blessings on students as they strive to be responsible people of God in every part of their life, dating included.

8. "i'd date him/her, but . . ."

my ideal date

I look for a date who is ...

___ attractive

___ caring

___ fun to be with

___ a good conversationalist

___ a person of faith

___ considerate of me (and others)

___ patient with their parents

___ popular

I look for a date who has ...

___ a good sense of humor

___ Christian values

___ a decent car

___ a great body

___ good grades

___ patience with young children

___ great looks

Looking at Marriage

Ephesians 5:22–28

"Wives, submit to your husbands as to the Lord."

"Husbands, love your wives, just as Christ loved the church and gave Himself up for her."

Looking ahead

1 Corinthians 6:13–20

1 Corinthians 13:4–13

Scripture quotations: NIV®. Used by permission of Zondervan.

marriage

LESSON FOCUS

Young people usually have a strong sense of justice. But these same young people are often unsure of who is to blame. They may be especially shortsighted when they are at fault. When life does not seem fair, they may be tempted to blame God.

GOSPEL FOCUS

Through Jesus, God grants forgiveness to repentant sinners for the times when they fail to trust in His promises. The Holy Spirit enables believers to depend on God and to confess that He is still at work—supporting His people and accomplishing His plans.

Lesson Outline

ACTIVITY	SUGGESTED TIME	MATERIALS NEEDED
It's Not Fair!	15 minutes	Newsprint, markers, index cards
That Was Then . . .	15 minutes	Copies of Student Page, Bibles
This Is Now	15 minutes	Copies of Student Page, ruled paper, Bibles
How Do I . . .?	10 minutes	Bibles
Closing	5 minutes	White construction paper/poster board

IT'S NOT FAIR! (15 MINUTES)

Before class, hang two or three pieces of newsprint on a bulletin board, easel, or wall. Label each "It's not fair when . . ." Have markers by each paper. Also, gather a variety of "arts and crafts" materials—markers, crayons, and heavy white paper or poster board for the closing activity.

Ask students to think about situations they've witnessed or experienced that seemed unfair. Ask them to list the situations on the newsprint. Be prepared to offer examples to get them started. Ask, "Why do you think the situation is unfair?"

Discuss with the class the unfair situations students listed. Create a continuum from 1–10 in the front of the classroom. Explain that students will need to decide how difficult it would be for them to accept each circumstance, without any negative feelings, using the scale, with 1 as having little or no trouble accepting and 10 as having a major problem accepting.

Or . . .

Discuss each of the situations the students have listed. As you do so, write each one on a separate index card. When all the situations have been written on cards, add a few "positive" experiences (being named in a rich uncle's will, someone buying you a new car, getting front-row seats at a favorite concert, etc.). Mix these in, shuffle the cards, and then deal one or more to each student. Have students role-play a possible response to the situation(s) they were dealt.

THAT WAS THEN . . . (15 MINUTES)

Whenever we deem something as unfair, we seem able to justify our opinion, blame someone else, or even blame God. Hand out the Student Page. Give students a chance to consider each of the people from the Bible and try to explain why each could easily have cried, "It's not fair." Seek a volunteer for each. Or, if your class is large, allow students to work in small groups. Ask, "Which of these individuals do you think had a legitimate reason to say, 'It's not fair!'? Which did not?" Explain your answer.

THIS IS NOW (15 MINUTES)

Say, "That's great for those people, but God worked differently back then. It was probably a lot easier to deal with the hardships and the struggles when God spoke to people directly. But this is today. What do we have to hang on to when life seems so unfair? Where do we begin?"

Read 2 Timothy 3:16. Then say, "God continues to speak directly to us today in His Word, the Bible. What does God say to us in His Word about struggles and hardships?" Allow time for students to offer suggestions. Then divide the class into small groups and assign each group one or more of the passages on the Student Page. Have each group paraphrase the main idea of the passage as if the author were talking to people today. Give them five to seven minutes to write their paraphrase. Then have volunteers address the rest of the group as a friend would, in an attempt to encourage or support them with this newfound wisdom.

After students have shared their paraphrase, say, "God's Word offers forgiveness through Jesus for the times we doubt God's activity in our life and for the times we blame Him for our troubles. His love and forgiveness enables us to approach hardships with confidence and hope."

BUT HOW DO I . . .? (10 MINUTES)

Ask, "How can we daily 'let go and let God'?" Check out Hebrews 10:23–24 for some practical suggestions.

Give students a few minutes in their small groups to discover the three suggestions.

1. "Hold unswervingly to the hope" of salvation through Christ, found in God's Word.

2. "Spur one another on toward love and good deeds" as you work by God's power to correct any unfairness you observe.

3. "Meeting together" in worship or "encourage one another" in all circumstances, especially in difficult times.

Emphasize that God's Word is the source of strength and hope found in each suggestion. God reveals His salvation through Christ in His Word. God tells how Christians are to treat one another in His Word. In worship God speaks to us in His Word.

CLOSING (5 MINUTES)

Give each participant a large piece of white construction paper. Using materials available, students are to design a collage or poster with a slogan or other catchy phrase to remind themselves of one of the truths they discovered today. It could be about God's promises to take care of us and work things out, even when we don't understand or it seems unfair. Encourage students to make their project eye-catching and colorful, but not to let their creativity get in the way of the message.

Or . . .

Design an encouraging Christian T-shirt based on this lesson, front only or front and back. What would it say? How about a visual design?

Close by asking about any specific concerns or frustrations that currently plague the participants or someone they know. Include these concerns in prayer.

9. Who's to blame?

that was then . . .

You think you've got it bad? Consider the following Bible characters. Pick one and tell why that person may have felt unfairly treated.

*Adam & Eve **(Genesis 3:23)***

*Cain **(Genesis 4:3–5)***

*Abel **(Genesis 4:8)***

*Esau **(Genesis 27:33–36)***

*Joseph **(Genesis 37:23–27)***

*Samson **(Judges 14:12–20)***

*Job **(Job 1:12–22; 2:6–8)***

*Daniel **(Daniel 6:1–16)***

*Paul and Silas **(Acts 16:16–24)***

this is now

Dear _____; I'd like to try to help . . .

*Write a paragraph or two paraphrasing the hope and encouragement you find in God's Word. Consider one or more of the following Scripture references: **Job 2:10; Isaiah 55:8–9; Proverbs 3:11–12; Romans 8:28; 1 Peter 3:17; 1 Corinthians 10:24; Hebrews 6:17–20; Hebrews 10:19–25; Hebrews 12:1–11.***

bUt hOW dO i . . .?

God in His mercy has not left us alone to deal with our concerns. In **Hebrews 10:23–25** God offers three suggestions by which Christians are strengthened to overcome difficulties—even events that seem unfair.

verse 23

verse 24

verse 25

10

kids having kids

LESSON FOCUS

Teenage pregnancy continues to be a significant problem in our society. God reveals in the Bible His plan for marriage and children and shows that sexual relationships outside of marriage are sinful.

GOSPEL FOCUS

God in His love for us through Christ offers forgiveness for all sin. He promised to work all things for the good of those who love Him. God will bring blessing out of the sin and sorrow of teen pregnancy. He helps young people make God-pleasing choices in this area as in all others. He also empowers them to share the reasons for those choices with others as they have opportunity.

Lesson Outline

LESSON ACTIVITY	SUGGESTED TIME	MATERIALS NEEDED
Opening	10 minutes	Teen-oriented magazines or several TV commercials on videotape
Ready? or NOT!	10 minutes	Copies of Student Page
A Look in The Book	30 minutes	Copies of Student Page, Bibles
Closing	5 minutes	None

A NOTE TO THE LEADER

Statistics suggest that some of the students in any group of young people will already be sexually active. Don't assume that all the youth in your class are exceptions to this rule. Deal with the matter of chastity frankly, but show love and concern for any who have already committed sexual sin. Show them that God is always ready to forgive those who repent of sin.

Teens 15–19-years-old gave birth to over 468,000 babies in the year 2000. However, the birth rate among teens has declined by as much as 29 percent in the last 10 years in some states. For more statistics about teen pregnancy see www.cdc.gov/nchs/fastats/teenbrth.htm.

You may have the opportunity to personally assist one or more young people during or after this study. Students may also be very helpful to one another during the discussion. Make yourself or another resource available for further private discussion and counsel for any who wish it. Allow time to provide care, comfort, and God's promises of forgiveness for hurting teens. Do not be afraid to explore answers and spend more time than suggested for each section. Additional support and information is available from Lutherans for Life (www.lutheransforlife.org).

OPENING (15 MINUTES)

Gather youth-oriented magazines, including typical choices for young men and women, such as *Sports Illustrated, YM, Seventeen,* and *Spin.* Or tape about six television commercials shown during programs directed at teens, such as sporting events, mid-afternoon soap operas, and evening sitcoms.

Begin this study by directing your students' attention to the magazines you have gathered or show the videotape you have made. Ask the students to look for commercial use of sexuality as a means of selling a product, noting especially the results, which are implied or promised. They will find many advertisements that seem to promise fun, adventure, excitement, and great relationships. The implication is that the results of freely expressing and acting on sexual feelings are all positive. Ask, "Are these accurate pictures of the results of free sexual expression? What things are not being addressed by the advertising media? What's missing?" Record any volunteered responses on newsprint or on a marker board. Include these if they are not mentioned: increased responsibility; risk of STDs; possibility of pregnancy and/or parenthood; emotional attachment; and conflict with parents.

Say, "The bottom line is this: society and media frequently give an incomplete picture of what sex is all about. They show the things that will sell, but withhold any information that does not achieve their purposes. Our goal today is to look at the whole picture."

READY? OR NOT! (10 MINUTES)

Invite your students individually to study the reality-check questions on the Student Page with words like these:

"The questions in this short quiz provide an opportunity for you to see how ready you are and how honest you are being with yourself, your peers, your boy/girl-friend, and God. You will not be required to share your responses to these questions. But I urge you to respond to them honestly. I will give you a few moments to do that now."

After a few moments, continue with words like these: "God's Word calls you to wait until you have committed yourself to another person in marriage before becoming sexually active. If you have not waited, know that God forgives those who confess their sin and, through the power of His forgiveness through Christ, can help you turn your life around and start over.

A LOOK IN THE BOOK (20 MINUTES)

Form groups of three to five students for discussion. Distribute copies of the Student Page. Tell students they will have about 5 minutes to prepare responses to the four questions.

After allowing time for discussion, invite volunteers to report for their group on each question. Use the following comments to assist you.

1. All the responses are possible. The most technically correct is the third one, that God created Eve specifically to fill a void in Adam's life. Without her, Adam could not fulfill God's intentions for His people.

2. "All of the above" and much more is implied in the union of Adam and Eve.

3. Adam and Eve are told to "increase in number" (have children) and to "subdue" and care for God's creation. Having children is a natural consequence of God's creation of Adam and Eve, male and female.

4. List the student responses on newsprint or on the board. Marriage involves commitment and faithfulness to each other and responsibility for spouse and children. Your students' responses may list many things that can be included in these two broad categories.

Read, or have a volunteer read, 1 Corinthians 6:12–20. Direct the small groups to share their responses to the questions that follow on the Student Page. After a few minutes invite small groups to share responses to each of the questions. Include the following comments in the discussion.

a. God created sexual activity for the "one flesh" union described in Genesis 2:24. It is a gift for the expression of love in marriage.

b. All sexuality outside of the one-flesh union is sexual immorality—sin. Sin is a demonstration of our natural rejection of God.

c. Sexual intercourse goes way beyond the other touching, sharing, and communicating that takes place between people. The Bible describes it as "two [becoming] one flesh." It is an intimate act, inappropriate between strangers or even close friends. Therefore, God condemns casual sex and prostitution.

d. Sexual attraction has a spiritual dimension. It is therefore subject to active assault by Satan. In addition, our human nature seems always open to sin.

e. and f. Paul makes a similar point with each of these phrases (and v. 15)— Christians have the power of Christ present in them through the Holy Spirit. Christ's power working in us enables us to resist the temptation to sin. His power assures us of the forgiveness Christ bought for us on the cross through His suffering and death. (See also Romans 6:6–14.)

Through this discussion, emphasize that God clearly has a goal for sex within marriage, not outside of it. God has given us sexual desire. He has given us His Son, Jesus, to ensure our forgiveness for all the ways in which we sin. He will also provide self-control so that by God's grace offered in His Word and Sacrament we may have mastery over our temptations.

Summarize by saying, "*Sexual attraction, marriage, sexual activity,* and *parenthood* are shown in the Bible as related activities. They form a progression." (Write the italicized words on newsprint or the board in order from left to right, with arrows pointing from each word or phrase to the one on its right.) Continue, "Not everyone will progress to every step. Some may not marry. Some married people will not have children. Nonetheless, they each form part of the whole picture. It is important to see the potential consequences of the sexual attraction that society displays so frequently.

"We know, however, that things do not always follow these steps. Each year unmarried teenagers give birth to about half a million babies. This is not God's plan. But these births result in many of the same consequences and responsibilities that usually come with marriage and family. What consequences can you identity that will result for unmarried teenage parents—males and females?"

On newsprint or the board, have students brainstorm a list of ways that becoming a teenage parent could alter a teen's life now and in the future. The list could include medical expenses, child support, quitting school, finding child-care, getting an entry-level job, blaming each other, and so forth.

CLOSING (5 MINUTES)

Say, "If you have not waited for sexual activity, know that God forgives those who confess their sin. Through the power of His forgiveness through Christ, He can help you turn your life around and start over. Listen to God's Word from Hebrews 10:22–24:

"'Let us draw near to God with a sincere heart in full assurance of faith, having our hearts sprinkled to cleanse us from a guilty conscience and having our bodies washed with pure water. Let us hold unswervingly to the hope we profess, for He who promised is faithful. And let us consider how we may spur one another on toward love and good deeds.'"

Close with a prayer. Thank God for the model of marriage and family He has provided. Ask forgiveness for our shortcomings in our relationship with Him and with others. Pray for strength to make new beginnings in relationships that are marred by sin.

10. teen parenthood: kids having kids

Ready? Or Not!

1. My greatest fear about having sex is (pregnancy, STDs, performance).

2. Am I responsible enough to handle the physical consequences of sex
(STDs, AIDS, parenthood, pregnancy)?

3. Am I responsible enough to handle the financial consequences of sex
(medical expenses, child support, spouse support, education, transportation, etc.)?

4. Am I responsible enough to handle the emotional consequences of sex
(guilt, disappointment, anxiety about pregnancy, emotional scars)?

5. Am I responsible enough to handle the spiritual consequences of sex
(in my relationship with God, in my relationship with my partner)?

a Look in the book

Read **Genesis 2:18–25.** Then respond to the following:

1. Adam and Eve became the first married couple because

___ it was love at first sight.

___ they were the only man and woman, so they had no other choice.

___ God created them to be together.

2. **Verse 24**, especially the words "united" and "one flesh," imply that

___ Adam and Eve were joined in marriage.

___ Adam and Eve had sexual relationships.

___ Adam and Eve shared responsibility and commitment for one another.

___ all of the above.

3. Read **Genesis 1:27–28.** What responsibilities did God give to Adam and Eve?

4. What other responsibilities are involved in marriage?

Read **1 Corinthians 6:12–20**. Discuss the following questions:

a. When is sex permissible?

b. When is sex not beneficial? Why not?

c. What happens when two people engage in sex?

d. Why is sexual control so difficult to practice?

e. What does it mean that "your body is a temple of the Holy Spirit"?

f. What does it mean that we have been "bought at a price"?

79

II

inadequate cash FLOW

LESSON FOCUS

"I have learned to be content whatever the circumstances" (Philippians 4:11). Paul's words challenge the modern notion that money can fix all of the world's ills and satisfy all of our personal needs and desires.

GOSPEL FOCUS

On the cross Jesus suffered the consequences for our discontent. As the Holy Spirit works through the Word to strengthen our faith, God empowers us to "be content whatever the circumstances." Jesus forgives us for our discontent.

Lesson Outline

ACTIVITY	SUGGESTED TIME	MATERIALS NEEDED
Take a Stand	10 minutes	"Disagree" and "Agree" signs
Contentment and Me	10 minutes	Copies of Student Page
Contentment and God's Word	15 minutes	Copies of Student Page, Bibles
My Contentment Motto	15 minutes	Copies of Student Page, Bibles
Thank You, Lord!	5 minutes	Copies of Student Page

TAKE A STAND (10 MINUTES)

Begin the session by saying, "Our session today deals with the subject of material things. Let's get a sense of how we feel about money and material goods." Have everyone stand. Designate one side of the room "Agree" and the other side "Disagree" with paper signs. Ask participants to move to indicate their agreement or disagreement as you read the following statements. As participants "take their stand" on each statement, you may want to ask one or two to explain why they've chosen to stand where they are.

* I'd rather be rich than smart.

* I'd rather be rich than famous.

* Money may not be the most important thing in the world, but it runs a close second.

* Money can buy happiness.

* My first priority in considering a profession is its earning potential.

* There's nothing wrong with wanting more, so long as it's not an obsession.

* If Jesus were alive today, He would condemn our preoccupation with financial success.

* The advantages of wealth far outweigh the disadvantages.

* Americans confuse their "needs" with their "wants."

Have students return to their seats. Then pray, "Lord, help us to grow and teach us Your will concerning financial and material concerns. In Jesus' name we pray. Amen."

CONTENTMENT AND ME (10 MINUTES)

Distribute a copy of the Student Page to each participant. Have students complete "I'd be happier if . . ." with as many responses as possible in two minutes. Then give them two minutes to complete the line "I'm thankful for . . ." Discuss their lists. Next, have students identify their sources of contentment. Categorize their responses as they are given under the following headings on newsprint or the chalkboard: material things, church/faith, social life, family, money, school, self/abilities, and other.

Tally their responses as a group. Ask, "How many items on your lists fit in the 'Material Things' category?" Have students hold up the corresponding number of fingers, and then record the total number next to "Material Things" on the categories sheet. Do the same for all categories on the sheet. Then ask, "What do our responses say about the sources of our contentment in our life?"

CONTENTMENT AND GOD'S WORD (15 MINUTES)

Say, "Let's see what God's Word has to say about contentment." As students work through the Bible-study portion of the Student Page, keep these things in mind and be ready to share them.

* Scripture is clear that the pleasures of this world are a gift from God to be enjoyed (Proverbs 3:9–10; 14:24; Malachi 3:8–10). They become sinful when they become more important to us than God (idolatry) or dangerous when they pull us away from Him and His desires for our lives. Because of sin, it is impossible for us to give God the priority He deserves. But the blood of Christ cleanses us from all sin, including the sin of idolatry. In faith, we daily confess our sin, gladly receive His forgiveness, and apprehend His power to do what He desires.

* Use of earthly blessings to give God glory include a tithe, helping the poor, offering a home for a church retreat, using your van to transport church groups, and so forth. God also provides us with a vocation; this includes the financial blessings that come with that vocation. The income from our vocation enables us to care for our families.

* Money can bring investment confusion and hassles, IRS audits, temptations (drugs, greed, party life, etc.), the loss of awareness of one's need for God, and so forth. Note: money is not evil in and of itself; it is the love of money that is sinful.

* Paul was content in God's strength, which had provided him salvation through Jesus' sacrifice on the cross. If time allows, you may want to discuss the concept of wants and needs further. The world teaches us to want. True contentment is the opposite—knowing that God will provide for all of our needs.

MY CONTENTMENT MOTTO (15 MINUTES)

Direct the students to the T-shirt on the Student Page. Say, "Reread 1 Timothy 6:6–10 and Philippians 4:11–13. Look for a verse or phrase that would make a good T-shirt slogan or design. Then sketch a design on the T-shirt picture on the Student Page." To help get the creative juices flowing, have one or two students share the phrase or verse they've chosen and let the group brainstorm ways to express it on a T-shirt. If time allows, provide markers or crayons and extra paper for students to complete the design.

THANK YOU, LORD! (5 MINUTES)

Pair participants and instruct them to go to a quiet place. (If this is not possible, sitting close together in the room is an option.) Ask them to spend a moment sharing with each other their "I'm thankful for . . ." lists. Then have them pray a prayer of thanks for their partner, mentioning to God the things for which their partner is grateful.

When they have finished praying in pairs, gather everyone together in a circle and have them join hands or link arms. Thank God again for His many blessings, especially His gift of forgiveness and eternal life through Jesus. Ask Him to help you to be content in any and every circumstance. Then have students repeat after you: "I can / do everything / through Him / who gives me strength!" Repeat this two or three times with increasing boldness before saying "Amen."

money

II. inadequate cash FLOW

contentment and me

I'd be happier if . . .

I'm thankful for . . .

contentment and god's word

Read **1 Timothy 6:6–10**. Reread **verse 7**. Circle the things in your lists that you cannot "take with you" when you die.

Is it wrong to find pleasure in the things of this world? If not, when does it become wrong? (See **Proverbs 3:9–10; 14:24; Malachi 3:8–10**.) List below the blessings money can bring that, when mixed with godliness and contentment, could give God glory. Reread also **1 Timothy 6:10**. List the "griefs" lots of money can bring.

Read **Philippians 4:11–13**. What was Paul's "secret of being content in any and every situation" (**v. 13**)? How does it apply to your life right now?

79

12

by my example

LESSON FOCUS

Many people serve as teachers and examples for youth. Young people can also serve as mentors and models, setting examples and giving support for faith growth and development to those younger than themselves. Youth pattern their life after the models they see, especially the older youth they see and know.

GOSPEL FOCUS

Young people can grow in their faith through the study of God's Word and through a close relationship with their Savior and Mentor, Jesus. God empowers young people through His Word and Sacraments to serve as models and mentors for others.

Lesson Outline

LESSON ACTIVITY	SUGGESTED TIME	MATERIALS NEEDED
Hero Collage	10 minutes	Magazines, poster board, scissors, and glue
Things That Influence Me	10 minutes	Paper and pencils or pens
Bible Models Puzzle	10 minutes	Copies of Student Page, Bibles
Bible Search	15 minutes	Copies of Student Page, Bibles
Situations for Discussion	10 minutes	Copies of Student Page
Closing	5 minutes	None

HERO COLLAGE (10 MINUTES)

Provide a stack of old *People, Time, Rolling Stone*, and *Sports Illustrated* magazines. Have students search for one or more pictures of the world's heroes. Have the group assemble and glue the pictures onto poster board as a collage. Then ask:

1. What makes these people heroes?

2. What would be the best part of being like them?

3. What challenges might you encounter if you were in their shoes?

As you discuss these questions, help students to see how these people become models for others.

THINGS THAT INFLUENCE ME (10 MINUTES)

Give each student a sheet of paper and a pen or pencil. Print the following topics on newsprint or on the board: my favorite television show, my favorite movie, my favorite song, my favorite subject in school, the best teacher I've ever had, and the most influential person at school. Ask students to list individually their responses to the topics and a few words about the impact each has had on their lives—something they have learned from or a quality they have admired in each.

Form groups of three to five students and allow them to share their responses. After about five minutes of sharing, invite a different volunteer to respond to each of the topics. Accept all answers. Note the kinds of impact these topics have on our lives.

BIBLE MODELS PUZZLE (10 MINUTES)

Distribute copies of the Student Page. Say, "Even our heroes had heroes and others who taught them." Invite students to work alone or in pairs to complete the puzzle by filling in the name of the mentor or role model for each of these biblical people.

Answer Key:

DOWN

1. Elijah

2. Lois and Eunice

3. Moses

ACROSS

4. Solomon

5. Jesus

6. Barnabas

BIBLE SEARCH (15 MINUTES)

Read or have a volunteer read 1 Timothy 4:12. Allow students to discuss the questions in their small groups for about five minutes. Then invite small groups to report on their answers. Incorporate the following comments.

1. We don't know exactly how old Timothy was. He may have been in his 20s or early 30s. Paul, though, makes a point about broadening the expectations of others by being a responsible example to others at an age when it is not yet expected.

by my example

2. Assisting in worship by ushering or lighting candles, visiting the elderly or sick, assisting with improvements to the church building, and many other ideas may be suggested.

3. Stress Paul's words, "set an example for the believers." Regular worship and Bible study; respect for others, especially those in authority; and being a worthy role model are possible answers. Students may suggest others.

4. The only power for such a lifestyle is found in Christ at work in us through the Holy Spirit in the Sacraments and the proclamation of God's Word.

If you have time, brainstorm a list of ways that you can set an example for those younger than you in each of the following areas. You might use a sheet of newsprint for each area listed below:

Speech

Lifestyle

Love

Faith

Purity

SITUATIONS FOR DISCUSSION (10 MINUTES)

As you have time, discuss one or more of the case studies in small groups or with the whole class. Encourage students to develop an attitude of service and responsibility toward those who are younger than themselves. Remind them of the support and strength they gain through worship and Bible study. Conclude with words like these:

"Witnessing is more than just talking about our faith. It is also the examples we set in the words we say and the actions we do. We have all failed to be the best examples all of the time. For this, there is a clear forgiveness through the suffering and death of Jesus Christ and the chance to start anew today with His power at work in us. Our lives are on display for the world to see. God is at work in our lives and will strengthen us to live for Him, even when we find it difficult."

CLOSING (5 MINUTES)

Allow the students to create the closing prayer. Encourage them to seek forgiveness for the times they've failed as models and mentors and to seek strength to be good examples.

12. by my example

bible models puzzle

Even our heroes had heroes and others who taught them. Complete the puzzle by filling in the name of the mentor or role model for each of these biblical people.

DOWN

1. *Elisha* **(1 Kings 19:16, 21; 2 Kings 2:5–14)**

2. *Timothy* **(2 Timothy 1:5; 3:14–15)**

3. *Joshua* **(Joshua 1:1–9)**

ACROSS

4. *Solomon's sons* **(Proverbs 4)**

5. *John* **(John 21:20–25)**

6. *Saul/Paul* **(Acts 9:19b–31)**

bible search

Read through **1 Timothy 4:12**.

1. What does this verse say about how old you need to be to help and serve one another?

2. What are some ways you can serve—right now?

3. How might you serve those who are two or three years younger than you as mentors or role models?

4. How is it possible to do these things? What can empower us?

situations for discussion

1. One of the active guys in your youth group at church is popular and widely respected at school and church. His girlfriend becomes pregnant. What kind of message might this give to the other youth? How might it affect younger youth? What can you do with him and for him? for both parents-to-be?

2. You overhear your best friend's little sister, a seventh-grade student, talking about going to the big party on Friday night. You have always gotten along well with her. How can you be a role model for her? How can you be her mentor (a person who encourages, teaches, and guides someone else) without turning her off? What might you say about your common faith in Christ?

3. You walk into the locker room and a small circle of younger students are standing around laughing and making comments about a sexually oriented picture and joke in a magazine. They see you enter and call you over. What can you do? What can you say? What effect could your action have on them? How is this a faith issue?

real DEAL
bible studies

available now!

IT'S YOUR DEAL—PERSONAL ISSUES

Tattooing/Body Piercing
Self-image
Maturity
Decision Making
Eating Disorders
Substance Abuse
Suicide
Anger
Leisure Time
College/Career
Personal Priorities
Opposite Sex

DEAL WITH IT!—SCHOOL ISSUES

School Violence
Bullying
Grades
Creation/Evolution (faith challenges)
Competition
Fitting In/Cliques
Stress
Cheating
Gangs
Date Abuse
Outcasts
Campus "Bible" Groups

PACKAGE DEAL—FAMILY ISSUES

Parents
Divorce
Family Conflict
Abuse
Blended/Nontraditional
Grief and Suffering
Co-dependency
Marriage
Blame
Teen Parenthood
Money
Mentors and Models

NO DEAL—TEMPTATIONS

Pornography
Sexual Boundaries
Temptations
Anger
Media
Television
Profanity
Gambling
"Little" Sins
Adultery
Sarcasm
Shame

available spring 2004

WHAT'S THE BIG DEAL?—WORLD ISSUES

Homosexuality/Alternative Lifestyles
HIV/AIDS
Bioethics (fetal tissue, stem cells, cloning)
Abortion
Euthanasia
Prejudice
Natural Disasters
Poverty
Terrorism
Environment
War
Peace

available spring 2004

IT'S A BIG DEAL!—FAITH ISSUES

Faith Challenges
Worship—Elements of Worship
Lutherans and Catholics
Nondenominational Churches
Lutherans and Other Christians
Judaism
Mormons
Jehovah's Witnesses
What Brand of Lutheran?
Religious Rites
Interpreting Scripture
Care Ministry/Servanting